D0286490

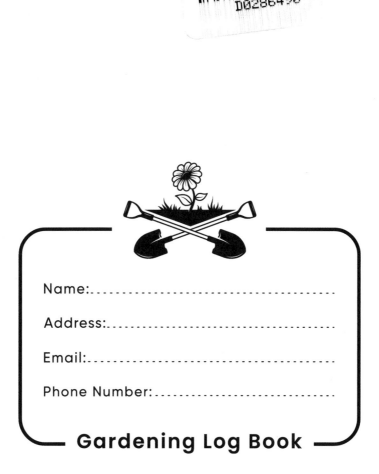

Name:..

Address:...

Email:...

Phone Number:.......................................

Gardening Log Book

NAME

LOCATION

SUPPLIER

PRICE

DATES

GERMINATED

PLANTED

HARVESTED

LIGHT LEVEL

☐ SUN   ☐ PARTIAL SUN

☐ SHADE   ☐ OTHER

FERTILISERS & EQUIPMENT

-	-
-	-

PLANTING INSTRUCTIONS

WATER REQUIREMENTS

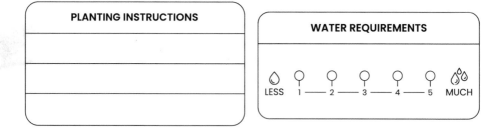

LESS   1 —— 2 —— 3 —— 4 —— 5   MUCH

CARE INSTRUCTIONS

STARTED FROM

☐ SEED   ☐ PLANT

RATING

SIZE	☆☆☆☆☆
COLOR	☆☆☆☆☆
TASTE	☆☆☆☆☆

SCIENTIFIC CLASS

☐ VEGETABLE	☐ FRUIT
☐ HERB	☐ FLOWER
☐ SHRUB	☐ TREE
☐ ANNUAL	☐ BIENNIAL
☐ PERENNIAL	☐ SEEDLING

ADDITIONAL NOTES

GARDEN LAYOUT

NAME

LOCATION

SUPPLIER

PRICE

DATES

GERMINATED

PLANTED

HARVESTED

LIGHT LEVEL

☐ SUN   ☐ PARTIAL SUN

☐ SHADE   ☐ OTHER

FERTILISERS & EQUIPMENT

-	-
-	-

PLANTING INSTRUCTIONS

WATER REQUIREMENTS

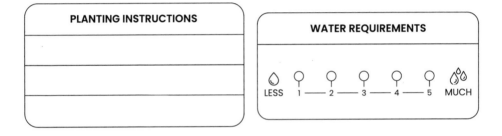

LESS 1 — 2 — 3 — 4 — 5 MUCH

CARE INSTRUCTIONS

STARTED FROM

☐ SEED   ☐ PLANT

SCIENTIFIC CLASS

☐ VEGETABLE	☐ FRUIT
☐ HERB	☐ FLOWER
☐ SHRUB	☐ TREE
☐ ANNUAL	☐ BIENNIAL
☐ PERENNIAL	☐ SEEDLING

RATING

SIZE ☆☆☆☆☆

COLOR ☆☆☆☆☆

TASTE ☆☆☆☆☆

ADDITIONAL NOTES

GARDEN LAYOUT

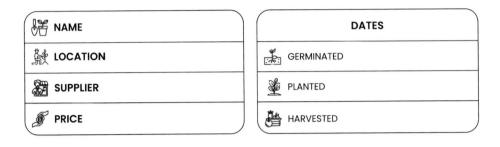 NAME		DATES

NAME
LOCATION
SUPPLIER
PRICE

DATES
GERMINATED
PLANTED
HARVESTED

LIGHT LEVEL

SUN	PARTIAL SUN
SHADE	OTHER

FERTILISERS & EQUIPMENT

-	-
-	-

PLANTING INSTRUCTIONS

WATER REQUIREMENTS

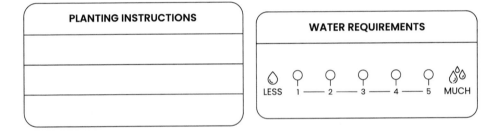

LESS 1 — 2 — 3 — 4 — 5 MUCH

CARE INSTRUCTIONS

STARTED FROM

SEED	PLANT

SCIENTIFIC CLASS

VEGETABLE	FRUIT
HERB	FLOWER
SHRUB	TREE
ANNUAL	BIENNIAL
PERENNIAL	SEEDLING

RATING

SIZE	☆☆☆☆☆
COLOR	☆☆☆☆☆
TASTE	☆☆☆☆☆

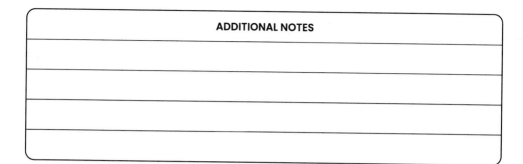

ADDITIONAL NOTES

GARDEN LAYOUT

🪴 NAME		**DATES**
🧑‍🌾 LOCATION		🌱 GERMINATED
🪴 SUPPLIER		🌿 PLANTED
💸 PRICE		🍅 HARVESTED

LIGHT LEVEL

☐ SUN	☐ PARTIAL SUN
☐ SHADE	☐ OTHER

FERTILISERS & EQUIPMENT

-	-
-	-

PLANTING INSTRUCTIONS

WATER REQUIREMENTS

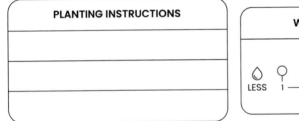

LESS   1 —— 2 —— 3 —— 4 —— 5   MUCH

CARE INSTRUCTIONS

STARTED FROM

☐ SEED	☐ PLANT

RATING

🪴 SIZE	☆☆☆☆☆
🍎 COLOR	☆☆☆☆☆
🍇 TASTE	☆☆☆☆☆

SCIENTIFIC CLASS

☐ VEGETABLE	☐ FRUIT
☐ HERB	☐ FLOWER
☐ SHRUB	☐ TREE
☐ ANNUAL	☐ BIENNIAL
☐ PERENNIAL	☐ SEEDLING

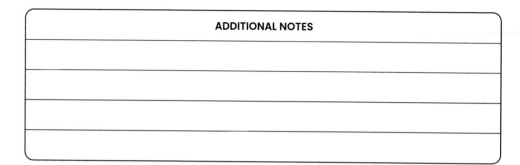

ADDITIONAL NOTES

GARDEN LAYOUT

NAME

LOCATION

SUPPLIER

PRICE

DATES

GERMINATED

PLANTED

HARVESTED

LIGHT LEVEL

☐ SUN	☐ PARTIAL SUN
☐ SHADE	☐ OTHER

FERTILISERS & EQUIPMENT

-	-
-	-

PLANTING INSTRUCTIONS

WATER REQUIREMENTS

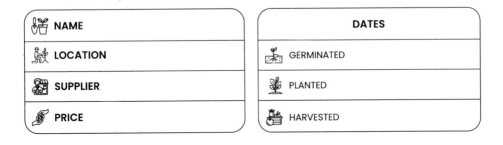

LESS 1 — 2 — 3 — 4 — 5 MUCH

CARE INSTRUCTIONS

STARTED FROM

☐ SEED	☐ PLANT

RATING

SIZE	☆☆☆☆☆
COLOR	☆☆☆☆☆
TASTE	☆☆☆☆☆

SCIENTIFIC CLASS

☐ VEGETABLE	☐ FRUIT
☐ HERB	☐ FLOWER
☐ SHRUB	☐ TREE
☐ ANNUAL	☐ BIENNIAL
☐ PERENNIAL	☐ SEEDLING

GARDEN LAYOUT

NAME

LOCATION

SUPPLIER

PRICE

DATES

GERMINATED

PLANTED

HARVESTED

LIGHT LEVEL

☐ SUN   ☐ PARTIAL SUN

☐ SHADE   ☐ OTHER

FERTILISERS & EQUIPMENT

-	-
-	-

PLANTING INSTRUCTIONS

WATER REQUIREMENTS

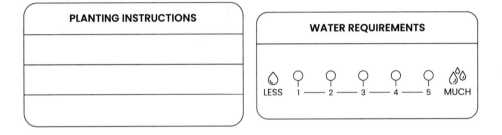

LESS   1 —— 2 —— 3 —— 4 —— 5   MUCH

CARE INSTRUCTIONS

STARTED FROM

☐ SEED   ☐ PLANT

SCIENTIFIC CLASS

☐ VEGETABLE	☐ FRUIT
☐ HERB	☐ FLOWER
☐ SHRUB	☐ TREE
☐ ANNUAL	☐ BIENNIAL
☐ PERENNIAL	☐ SEEDLING

RATING

SIZE	☆☆☆☆☆
COLOR	☆☆☆☆☆
TASTE	☆☆☆☆☆

GARDEN LAYOUT

NAME

LOCATION

SUPPLIER

PRICE

DATES

GERMINATED

PLANTED

HARVESTED

LIGHT LEVEL

| ☐ SUN | ☐ PARTIAL SUN |
| ☐ SHADE | ☐ OTHER |

FERTILISERS & EQUIPMENT

-	-
-	-

PLANTING INSTRUCTIONS

WATER REQUIREMENTS

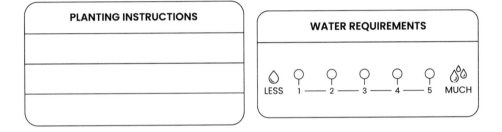

LESS 1 — 2 — 3 — 4 — 5 MUCH

CARE INSTRUCTIONS

STARTED FROM

| ☐ SEED | ☐ PLANT |

SCIENTIFIC CLASS

☐ VEGETABLE	☐ FRUIT
☐ HERB	☐ FLOWER
☐ SHRUB	☐ TREE
☐ ANNUAL	☐ BIENNIAL
☐ PERENNIAL	☐ SEEDLING

RATING

SIZE	☆☆☆☆☆
COLOR	☆☆☆☆☆
TASTE	☆☆☆☆☆

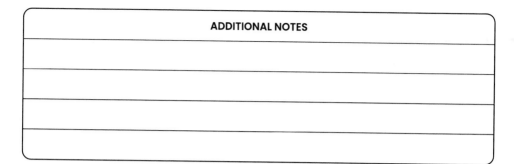

GARDEN LAYOUT

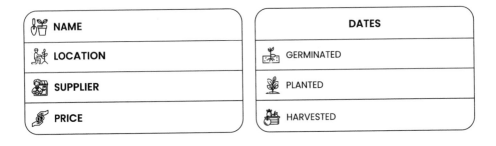

🪴 NAME		DATES
🧑‍🌾 LOCATION		🌱 GERMINATED
🎁 SUPPLIER		🌿 PLANTED
🤲 PRICE		🧺 HARVESTED

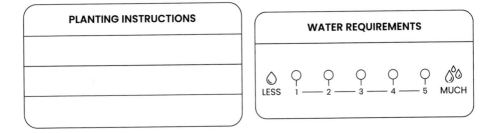

LIGHT LEVEL

☐ SUN   ☐ PARTIAL SUN

☐ SHADE   ☐ OTHER

FERTILISERS & EQUIPMENT

-	-
-	-

PLANTING INSTRUCTIONS

WATER REQUIREMENTS

💧   ○   ○   ○   ○   ○   💧💧

LESS   1 — 2 — 3 — 4 — 5   MUCH

CARE INSTRUCTIONS

STARTED FROM

☐ SEED   ☐ PLANT

RATING

📟 SIZE	☆☆☆☆☆
🍎 COLOR	☆☆☆☆☆
🍓 TASTE	☆☆☆☆☆

SCIENTIFIC CLASS

☐ VEGETABLE	☐ FRUIT
☐ HERB	☐ FLOWER
☐ SHRUB	☐ TREE
☐ ANNUAL	☐ BIENNIAL
☐ PERENNIAL	☐ SEEDLING

GARDEN LAYOUT

NAME

LOCATION

SUPPLIER

PRICE

DATES

GERMINATED

PLANTED

HARVESTED

LIGHT LEVEL

☐ SUN ☐ PARTIAL SUN

☐ SHADE ☐ OTHER

FERTILISERS & EQUIPMENT

-	-
-	-

PLANTING INSTRUCTIONS

WATER REQUIREMENTS

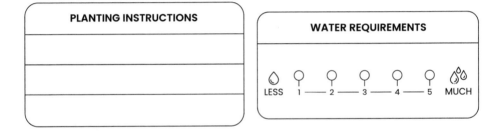

LESS 1 — 2 — 3 — 4 — 5 MUCH

CARE INSTRUCTIONS

STARTED FROM

☐ SEED ☐ PLANT

SCIENTIFIC CLASS

☐ VEGETABLE	☐ FRUIT
☐ HERB	☐ FLOWER
☐ SHRUB	☐ TREE
☐ ANNUAL	☐ BIENNIAL
☐ PERENNIAL	☐ SEEDLING

RATING

SIZE ☆☆☆☆☆

COLOR ☆☆☆☆☆

TASTE ☆☆☆☆☆

ADDITIONAL NOTES

GARDEN LAYOUT

🪴 NAME

🧑‍🌾 LOCATION

🪴 SUPPLIER

🧽 PRICE

DATES

🌱 GERMINATED

🌿 PLANTED

🧺 HARVESTED

LIGHT LEVEL

☐ SUN	☐ PARTIAL SUN
☐ SHADE	☐ OTHER

FERTILISERS & EQUIPMENT

-	-
-	-

PLANTING INSTRUCTIONS

WATER REQUIREMENTS

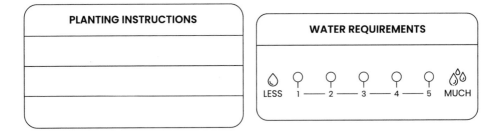

LESS 1 — 2 — 3 — 4 — 5 MUCH

CARE INSTRUCTIONS

STARTED FROM

☐ SEED	☐ PLANT

SCIENTIFIC CLASS

☐ VEGETABLE	☐ FRUIT
☐ HERB	☐ FLOWER
☐ SHRUB	☐ TREE
☐ ANNUAL	☐ BIENNIAL
☐ PERENNIAL	☐ SEEDLING

RATING

🌽 SIZE	☆☆☆☆☆
🍑 COLOR	☆☆☆☆☆
🍄 TASTE	☆☆☆☆☆

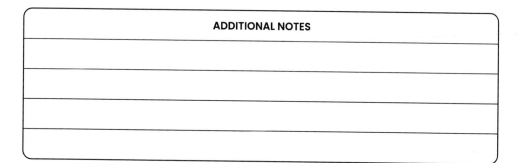

GARDEN LAYOUT

🌱 NAME		DATES

🌱 NAME
🪑 LOCATION
🧺 SUPPLIER
💰 PRICE

DATES
🌱 GERMINATED
🌿 PLANTED
🧺 HARVESTED

LIGHT LEVEL

☐ SUN	☐ PARTIAL SUN
☐ SHADE	☐ OTHER

FERTILISERS & EQUIPMENT

-	-
-	-

PLANTING INSTRUCTIONS

WATER REQUIREMENTS

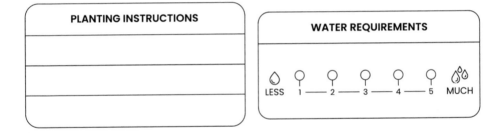

LESS 1 — 2 — 3 — 4 — 5 MUCH

CARE INSTRUCTIONS

STARTED FROM

☐ SEED	☐ PLANT

SCIENTIFIC CLASS

☐ VEGETABLE	☐ FRUIT
☐ HERB	☐ FLOWER
☐ SHRUB	☐ TREE
☐ ANNUAL	☐ BIENNIAL
☐ PERENNIAL	☐ SEEDLING

RATING

🪴 SIZE	☆☆☆☆☆
🍎 COLOR	☆☆☆☆☆
🫐 TASTE	☆☆☆☆☆

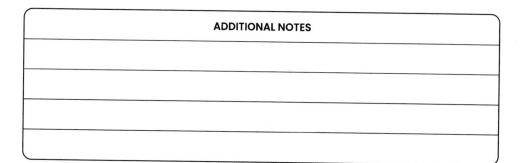

GARDEN LAYOUT

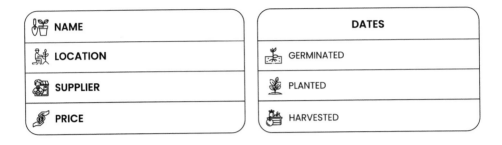

NAME	DATES
LOCATION	GERMINATED
SUPPLIER	PLANTED
PRICE	HARVESTED

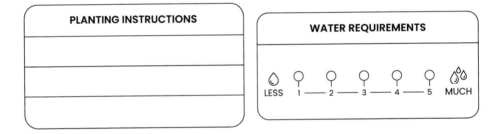

LIGHT LEVEL

☐ SUN	☐ PARTIAL SUN
☐ SHADE	☐ OTHER

FERTILISERS & EQUIPMENT

-	-
-	-

PLANTING INSTRUCTIONS

WATER REQUIREMENTS

LESS 1 — 2 — 3 — 4 — 5 MUCH

CARE INSTRUCTIONS

STARTED FROM

☐ SEED	☐ PLANT

RATING

🌶 SIZE	☆☆☆☆☆
🍎 COLOR	☆☆☆☆☆
🍓 TASTE	☆☆☆☆☆

SCIENTIFIC CLASS

☐ VEGETABLE	☐ FRUIT
☐ HERB	☐ FLOWER
☐ SHRUB	☐ TREE
☐ ANNUAL	☐ BIENNIAL
☐ PERENNIAL	☐ SEEDLING

ADDITIONAL NOTES

GARDEN LAYOUT

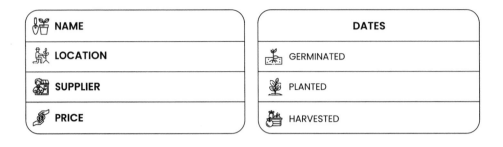 **NAME**	**DATES**
LOCATION	**GERMINATED**
SUPPLIER	**PLANTED**
PRICE	**HARVESTED**

LIGHT LEVEL

☐ SUN	☐ PARTIAL SUN
☐ SHADE	☐ OTHER

FERTILISERS & EQUIPMENT

-	-
-	-

PLANTING INSTRUCTIONS

WATER REQUIREMENTS

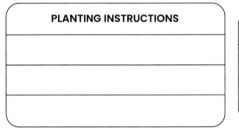

LESS 1 — 2 — 3 — 4 — 5 MUCH

CARE INSTRUCTIONS

STARTED FROM

☐ SEED	☐ PLANT

RATING

SIZE	☆☆☆☆☆
COLOR	☆☆☆☆☆
TASTE	☆☆☆☆☆

SCIENTIFIC CLASS

☐ VEGETABLE	☐ FRUIT
☐ HERB	☐ FLOWER
☐ SHRUB	☐ TREE
☐ ANNUAL	☐ BIENNIAL
☐ PERENNIAL	☐ SEEDLING

GARDEN LAYOUT

NAME

LOCATION

SUPPLIER

PRICE

DATES

GERMINATED

PLANTED

HARVESTED

LIGHT LEVEL

☐ SUN   ☐ PARTIAL SUN

☐ SHADE   ☐ OTHER

FERTILISERS & EQUIPMENT

-	-
-	-

PLANTING INSTRUCTIONS

WATER REQUIREMENTS

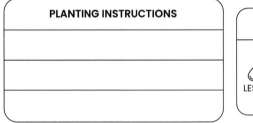

LESS   1 — 2 — 3 — 4 — 5   MUCH

CARE INSTRUCTIONS

STARTED FROM

☐ SEED   ☐ PLANT

SCIENTIFIC CLASS

☐ VEGETABLE   ☐ FRUIT

☐ HERB   ☐ FLOWER

☐ SHRUB   ☐ TREE

☐ ANNUAL   ☐ BIENNIAL

☐ PERENNIAL   ☐ SEEDLING

RATING

SIZE   ☆☆☆☆☆

COLOR   ☆☆☆☆☆

TASTE   ☆☆☆☆☆

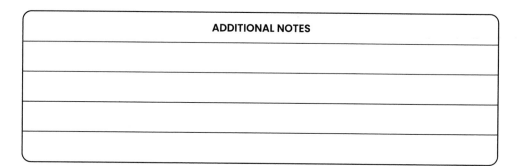

ADDITIONAL NOTES

GARDEN LAYOUT

NAME

LOCATION

SUPPLIER

PRICE

DATES

GERMINATED

PLANTED

HARVESTED

LIGHT LEVEL

☐ SUN	☐ PARTIAL SUN
☐ SHADE	☐ OTHER

FERTILISERS & EQUIPMENT

-	-
-	-

PLANTING INSTRUCTIONS

WATER REQUIREMENTS

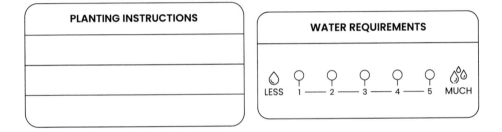

LESS 1 — 2 — 3 — 4 — 5 MUCH

CARE INSTRUCTIONS

STARTED FROM

☐ SEED	☐ PLANT

SCIENTIFIC CLASS

☐ VEGETABLE	☐ FRUIT
☐ HERB	☐ FLOWER
☐ SHRUB	☐ TREE
☐ ANNUAL	☐ BIENNIAL
☐ PERENNIAL	☐ SEEDLING

RATING

SIZE	☆☆☆☆☆
COLOR	☆☆☆☆☆
TASTE	☆☆☆☆☆

GARDEN LAYOUT

NAME

LOCATION

SUPPLIER

PRICE

DATES

GERMINATED

PLANTED

HARVESTED

LIGHT LEVEL

☐ SUN ☐ PARTIAL SUN

☐ SHADE ☐ OTHER

FERTILISERS & EQUIPMENT

-	-
-	-

PLANTING INSTRUCTIONS

WATER REQUIREMENTS

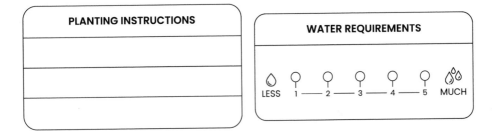

LESS 1 — 2 — 3 — 4 — 5 MUCH

CARE INSTRUCTIONS

STARTED FROM

☐ SEED ☐ PLANT

SCIENTIFIC CLASS

☐ VEGETABLE	☐ FRUIT
☐ HERB	☐ FLOWER
☐ SHRUB	☐ TREE
☐ ANNUAL	☐ BIENNIAL
☐ PERENNIAL	☐ SEEDLING

RATING

SIZE	☆☆☆☆☆
COLOR	☆☆☆☆☆
TASTE	☆☆☆☆☆

GARDEN LAYOUT

NAME

LOCATION

SUPPLIER

PRICE

DATES

GERMINATED

PLANTED

HARVESTED

LIGHT LEVEL

☐ SUN ☐ PARTIAL SUN

☐ SHADE ☐ OTHER

FERTILISERS & EQUIPMENT

-	-
-	-

PLANTING INSTRUCTIONS

WATER REQUIREMENTS

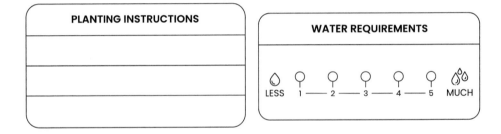

LESS 1 — 2 — 3 — 4 — 5 MUCH

CARE INSTRUCTIONS

STARTED FROM

☐ SEED ☐ PLANT

RATING

SIZE		☆☆☆☆☆
COLOR		☆☆☆☆☆
TASTE		☆☆☆☆☆

SCIENTIFIC CLASS

☐ VEGETABLE	☐ FRUIT
☐ HERB	☐ FLOWER
☐ SHRUB	☐ TREE
☐ ANNUAL	☐ BIENNIAL
☐ PERENNIAL	☐ SEEDLING

ADDITIONAL NOTES

GARDEN LAYOUT

NAME

LOCATION

SUPPLIER

PRICE

DATES

GERMINATED

PLANTED

HARVESTED

LIGHT LEVEL

☐ SUN   ☐ PARTIAL SUN

☐ SHADE   ☐ OTHER

FERTILISERS & EQUIPMENT

-	-
-	-

PLANTING INSTRUCTIONS

WATER REQUIREMENTS

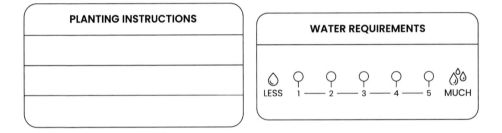

LESS 1 —— 2 —— 3 —— 4 —— 5 MUCH

CARE INSTRUCTIONS

STARTED FROM

☐ SEED	☐ PLANT

RATING

SIZE   ☆☆☆☆☆

COLOR ☆☆☆☆☆

TASTE ☆☆☆☆☆

SCIENTIFIC CLASS

☐ VEGETABLE	☐ FRUIT
☐ HERB	☐ FLOWER
☐ SHRUB	☐ TREE
☐ ANNUAL	☐ BIENNIAL
☐ PERENNIAL	☐ SEEDLING

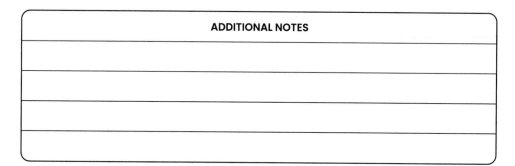

ADDITIONAL NOTES

GARDEN LAYOUT

NAME

LOCATION

SUPPLIER

PRICE

DATES

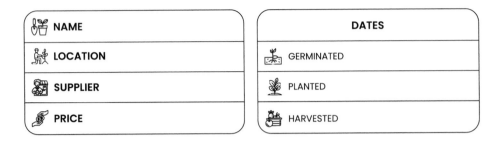

GERMINATED

PLANTED

HARVESTED

LIGHT LEVEL

☐ SUN ☐ PARTIAL SUN

☐ SHADE ☐ OTHER

FERTILISERS & EQUIPMENT

-	-
-	-

PLANTING INSTRUCTIONS

WATER REQUIREMENTS

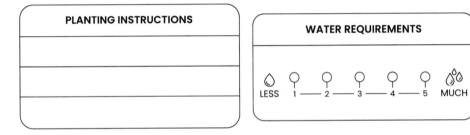

LESS 1 — 2 — 3 — 4 — 5 MUCH

CARE INSTRUCTIONS

STARTED FROM

☐ SEED ☐ PLANT

SCIENTIFIC CLASS

☐ VEGETABLE	☐ FRUIT
☐ HERB	☐ FLOWER
☐ SHRUB	☐ TREE
☐ ANNUAL	☐ BIENNIAL
☐ PERENNIAL	☐ SEEDLING

RATING

SIZE ☆☆☆☆☆

COLOR ☆☆☆☆☆

TASTE ☆☆☆☆☆

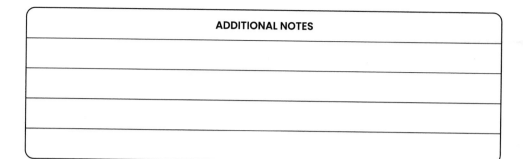

ADDITIONAL NOTES

GARDEN LAYOUT

NAME	DATES
LOCATION	GERMINATED
SUPPLIER	PLANTED
PRICE	HARVESTED

LIGHT LEVEL

☐ SUN	☐ PARTIAL SUN
☐ SHADE	☐ OTHER

FERTILISERS & EQUIPMENT

-	-
-	-

PLANTING INSTRUCTIONS

WATER REQUIREMENTS

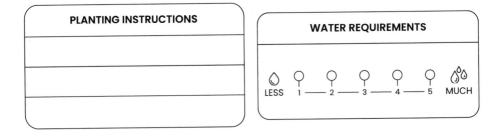

LESS   1 —— 2 —— 3 —— 4 —— 5   MUCH

CARE INSTRUCTIONS

STARTED FROM

☐ SEED	☐ PLANT

RATING

SIZE	☆☆☆☆☆
COLOR	☆☆☆☆☆
TASTE	☆☆☆☆☆

SCIENTIFIC CLASS

☐ VEGETABLE	☐ FRUIT
☐ HERB	☐ FLOWER
☐ SHRUB	☐ TREE
☐ ANNUAL	☐ BIENNIAL
☐ PERENNIAL	☐ SEEDLING

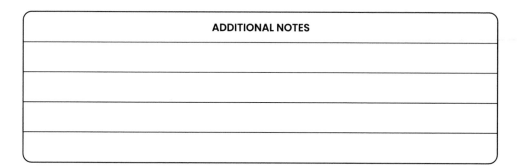

ADDITIONAL NOTES

GARDEN LAYOUT

NAME

LOCATION

SUPPLIER

PRICE

DATES

GERMINATED

PLANTED

HARVESTED

LIGHT LEVEL

☐ SUN ☐ PARTIAL SUN

☐ SHADE ☐ OTHER

FERTILISERS & EQUIPMENT

-	-
-	-

PLANTING INSTRUCTIONS

WATER REQUIREMENTS

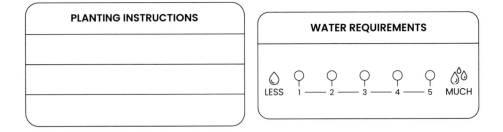

LESS 1 — 2 — 3 — 4 — 5 MUCH

CARE INSTRUCTIONS

STARTED FROM

☐ SEED ☐ PLANT

RATING

SIZE ☆☆☆☆☆

COLOR ☆☆☆☆☆

TASTE ☆☆☆☆☆

SCIENTIFIC CLASS

☐ VEGETABLE ☐ FRUIT

☐ HERB ☐ FLOWER

☐ SHRUB ☐ TREE

☐ ANNUAL ☐ BIENNIAL

☐ PERENNIAL ☐ SEEDLING

GARDEN LAYOUT

🪴 NAME		**DATES**	
🧑‍🌾 LOCATION		🌱 GERMINATED	
🪴 SUPPLIER		🌿 PLANTED	
💸 PRICE		🧺 HARVESTED	

LIGHT LEVEL	
☐ SUN	☐ PARTIAL SUN
☐ SHADE	☐ OTHER

FERTILISERS & EQUIPMENT	
-	-
-	-

PLANTING INSTRUCTIONS

WATER REQUIREMENTS

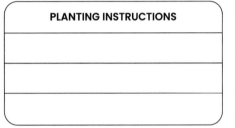

LESS 1 — 2 — 3 — 4 — 5 MUCH

CARE INSTRUCTIONS

STARTED FROM	
☐ SEED	☐ PLANT

RATING	
🪴 SIZE	☆☆☆☆☆
🍎 COLOR	☆☆☆☆☆
🫐 TASTE	☆☆☆☆☆

SCIENTIFIC CLASS	
☐ VEGETABLE	☐ FRUIT
☐ HERB	☐ FLOWER
☐ SHRUB	☐ TREE
☐ ANNUAL	☐ BIENNIAL
☐ PERENNIAL	☐ SEEDLING

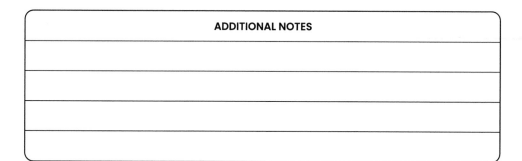

ADDITIONAL NOTES

GARDEN LAYOUT

NAME

LOCATION

SUPPLIER

PRICE

DATES

GERMINATED

PLANTED

HARVESTED

LIGHT LEVEL

- [ ] SUN
- [ ] PARTIAL SUN
- [ ] SHADE
- [ ] OTHER

FERTILISERS & EQUIPMENT

-	-
-	-

PLANTING INSTRUCTIONS

WATER REQUIREMENTS

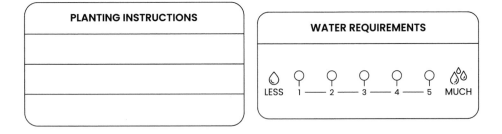

LESS 1 — 2 — 3 — 4 — 5 MUCH

CARE INSTRUCTIONS

STARTED FROM

- [ ] SEED
- [ ] PLANT

SCIENTIFIC CLASS

- [ ] VEGETABLE
- [ ] FRUIT
- [ ] HERB
- [ ] FLOWER
- [ ] SHRUB
- [ ] TREE
- [ ] ANNUAL
- [ ] BIENNIAL
- [ ] PERENNIAL
- [ ] SEEDLING

RATING

SIZE ☆☆☆☆☆

COLOR ☆☆☆☆☆

TASTE ☆☆☆☆☆

GARDEN LAYOUT

NAME

LOCATION

SUPPLIER

PRICE

DATES

GERMINATED

PLANTED

HARVESTED

LIGHT LEVEL

☐ SUN   ☐ PARTIAL SUN

☐ SHADE   ☐ OTHER

FERTILISERS & EQUIPMENT

-	-
-	-

PLANTING INSTRUCTIONS

WATER REQUIREMENTS

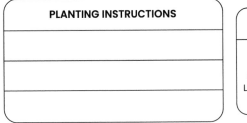

LESS   1 — 2 — 3 — 4 — 5   MUCH

CARE INSTRUCTIONS

STARTED FROM

☐ SEED   ☐ PLANT

SCIENTIFIC CLASS

☐ VEGETABLE	☐ FRUIT
☐ HERB	☐ FLOWER
☐ SHRUB	☐ TREE
☐ ANNUAL	☐ BIENNIAL
☐ PERENNIAL	☐ SEEDLING

RATING

SIZE   ☆☆☆☆☆

COLOR ☆☆☆☆☆

TASTE ☆☆☆☆☆

ADDITIONAL NOTES

GARDEN LAYOUT

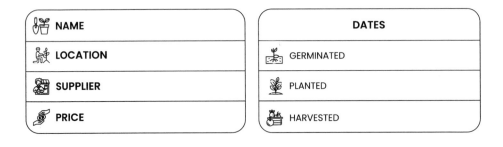

🪴 **NAME**	**DATES**
🧑‍🌾 **LOCATION**	🌱 GERMINATED
🛒 **SUPPLIER**	🌿 PLANTED
🌿 **PRICE**	🧺 HARVESTED

LIGHT LEVEL

☐ SUN	☐ PARTIAL SUN
☐ SHADE	☐ OTHER

FERTILISERS & EQUIPMENT

-	-
-	-

PLANTING INSTRUCTIONS

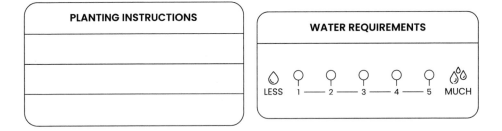

WATER REQUIREMENTS

LESS 1 — 2 — 3 — 4 — 5 MUCH

CARE INSTRUCTIONS

STARTED FROM

☐ SEED	☐ PLANT

RATING

🏷️ SIZE	☆☆☆☆☆
🍑 COLOR	☆☆☆☆☆
🍓 TASTE	☆☆☆☆☆

SCIENTIFIC CLASS

☐ VEGETABLE	☐ FRUIT
☐ HERB	☐ FLOWER
☐ SHRUB	☐ TREE
☐ ANNUAL	☐ BIENNIAL
☐ PERENNIAL	☐ SEEDLING

GARDEN LAYOUT

🪴 NAME	
🧑‍🌾 LOCATION	
🌱 SUPPLIER	
💰 PRICE	

DATES

🌱 GERMINATED
🌿 PLANTED
🪴 HARVESTED

LIGHT LEVEL

☐ SUN	☐ PARTIAL SUN
☐ SHADE	☐ OTHER

FERTILISERS & EQUIPMENT

-	-
-	-

PLANTING INSTRUCTIONS

WATER REQUIREMENTS

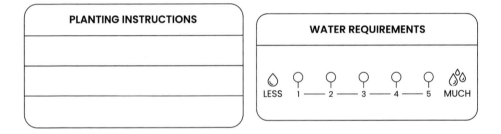

LESS 1 — 2 — 3 — 4 — 5 MUCH

CARE INSTRUCTIONS

STARTED FROM

☐ SEED	☐ PLANT

SCIENTIFIC CLASS

☐ VEGETABLE	☐ FRUIT
☐ HERB	☐ FLOWER
☐ SHRUB	☐ TREE
☐ ANNUAL	☐ BIENNIAL
☐ PERENNIAL	☐ SEEDLING

RATING

🌽 SIZE	☆☆☆☆☆
🍅 COLOR	☆☆☆☆☆
🫐 TASTE	☆☆☆☆☆

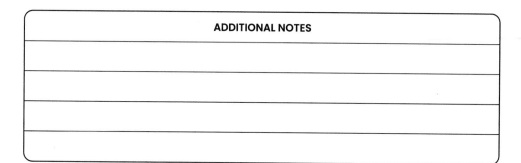

GARDEN LAYOUT

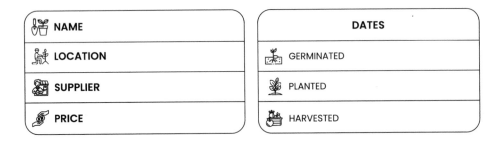

NAME

LOCATION

SUPPLIER

PRICE

DATES

GERMINATED

PLANTED

HARVESTED

LIGHT LEVEL

☐ SUN ☐ PARTIAL SUN

☐ SHADE ☐ OTHER

FERTILISERS & EQUIPMENT

-	-
-	-

PLANTING INSTRUCTIONS

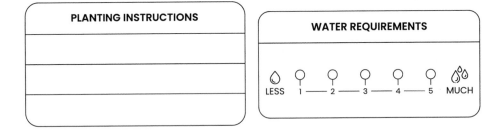

WATER REQUIREMENTS

LESS 1 — 2 — 3 — 4 — 5 MUCH

CARE INSTRUCTIONS

STARTED FROM

☐ SEED ☐ PLANT

SCIENTIFIC CLASS

☐ VEGETABLE	☐ FRUIT
☐ HERB	☐ FLOWER
☐ SHRUB	☐ TREE
☐ ANNUAL	☐ BIENNIAL
☐ PERENNIAL	☐ SEEDLING

RATING

SIZE	☆☆☆☆☆
COLOR	☆☆☆☆☆
TASTE	☆☆☆☆☆

ADDITIONAL NOTES

GARDEN LAYOUT

🪴 NAME	
🧑‍🌾 LOCATION	
🌱 SUPPLIER	
🤲 PRICE	

DATES

🌱 GERMINATED	
🌿 PLANTED	
🧺 HARVESTED	

LIGHT LEVEL

☐ SUN	☐ PARTIAL SUN
☐ SHADE	☐ OTHER

FERTILISERS & EQUIPMENT

-	-
-	-

PLANTING INSTRUCTIONS

WATER REQUIREMENTS

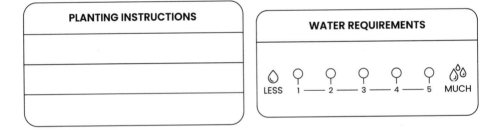

LESS 1 — 2 — 3 — 4 — 5 MUCH

CARE INSTRUCTIONS

STARTED FROM

☐ SEED	☐ PLANT

RATING

🧪 SIZE	☆☆☆☆☆
🍎 COLOR	☆☆☆☆☆
🫐 TASTE	☆☆☆☆☆

SCIENTIFIC CLASS

☐ VEGETABLE	☐ FRUIT
☐ HERB	☐ FLOWER
☐ SHRUB	☐ TREE
☐ ANNUAL	☐ BIENNIAL
☐ PERENNIAL	☐ SEEDLING

ADDITIONAL NOTES

GARDEN LAYOUT

NAME

LOCATION

SUPPLIER

PRICE

DATES

GERMINATED

PLANTED

HARVESTED

LIGHT LEVEL

☐ SUN ☐ PARTIAL SUN

☐ SHADE ☐ OTHER

FERTILISERS & EQUIPMENT

-	-
-	-

PLANTING INSTRUCTIONS

WATER REQUIREMENTS

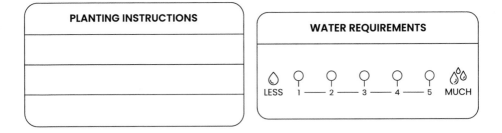

LESS 1 — 2 — 3 — 4 — 5 MUCH

CARE INSTRUCTIONS

STARTED FROM

☐ SEED ☐ PLANT

RATING

SIZE	☆☆☆☆☆	
COLOR	☆☆☆☆☆	
TASTE	☆☆☆☆☆	

SCIENTIFIC CLASS

☐ VEGETABLE ☐ FRUIT

☐ HERB ☐ FLOWER

☐ SHRUB ☐ TREE

☐ ANNUAL ☐ BIENNIAL

☐ PERENNIAL ☐ SEEDLING

ADDITIONAL NOTES

GARDEN LAYOUT

NAME

LOCATION

SUPPLIER

PRICE

DATES

GERMINATED

PLANTED

HARVESTED

LIGHT LEVEL

☐ SUN   ☐ PARTIAL SUN

☐ SHADE   ☐ OTHER

FERTILISERS & EQUIPMENT

-	-
-	-

PLANTING INSTRUCTIONS

WATER REQUIREMENTS

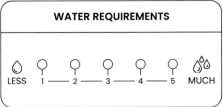

LESS   1 —— 2 —— 3 —— 4 —— 5   MUCH

CARE INSTRUCTIONS

STARTED FROM

☐ SEED	☐ PLANT

SCIENTIFIC CLASS

☐ VEGETABLE	☐ FRUIT
☐ HERB	☐ FLOWER
☐ SHRUB	☐ TREE
☐ ANNUAL	☐ BIENNIAL
☐ PERENNIAL	☐ SEEDLING

RATING

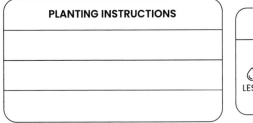

SIZE   ☆☆☆☆☆

COLOR ☆☆☆☆☆

TASTE ☆☆☆☆☆

ADDITIONAL NOTES

GARDEN LAYOUT

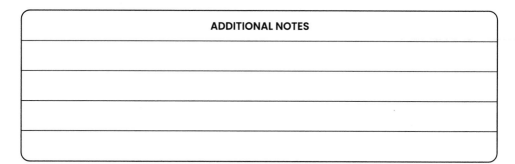

NAME	
LOCATION	
SUPPLIER	
PRICE	

DATES

GERMINATED	
PLANTED	
HARVESTED	

LIGHT LEVEL

☐ SUN	☐ PARTIAL SUN
☐ SHADE	☐ OTHER

FERTILISERS & EQUIPMENT

-	-
-	-

PLANTING INSTRUCTIONS

WATER REQUIREMENTS

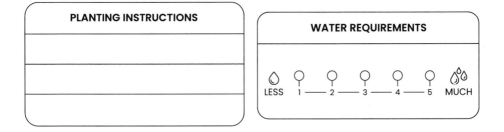

LESS 1 — 2 — 3 — 4 — 5 MUCH

CARE INSTRUCTIONS

STARTED FROM

☐ SEED	☐ PLANT

SCIENTIFIC CLASS

☐ VEGETABLE	☐ FRUIT
☐ HERB	☐ FLOWER
☐ SHRUB	☐ TREE
☐ ANNUAL	☐ BIENNIAL
☐ PERENNIAL	☐ SEEDLING

RATING

SIZE	☆☆☆☆☆
COLOR	☆☆☆☆☆
TASTE	☆☆☆☆☆

ADDITIONAL NOTES

GARDEN LAYOUT

NAME
LOCATION
SUPPLIER
PRICE

DATES
GERMINATED
PLANTED
HARVESTED

LIGHT LEVEL

☐ SUN	☐ PARTIAL SUN
☐ SHADE	☐ OTHER

FERTILISERS & EQUIPMENT

-	-
-	-

PLANTING INSTRUCTIONS

WATER REQUIREMENTS

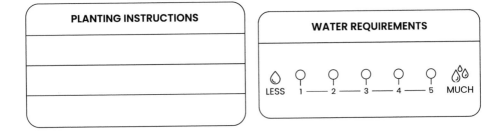

LESS 1 — 2 — 3 — 4 — 5 MUCH

CARE INSTRUCTIONS

STARTED FROM

☐ SEED	☐ PLANT

RATING

SIZE	☆☆☆☆☆
COLOR	☆☆☆☆☆
TASTE	☆☆☆☆☆

SCIENTIFIC CLASS

☐ VEGETABLE	☐ FRUIT
☐ HERB	☐ FLOWER
☐ SHRUB	☐ TREE
☐ ANNUAL	☐ BIENNIAL
☐ PERENNIAL	☐ SEEDLING

ADDITIONAL NOTES

GARDEN LAYOUT

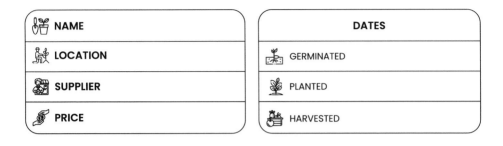 NAME	DATES

🪴 NAME
🧑‍🌾 LOCATION
🏪 SUPPLIER
💸 PRICE

DATES	
🌱 GERMINATED	
🌿 PLANTED	
🧺 HARVESTED	

LIGHT LEVEL

☐ SUN	☐ PARTIAL SUN
☐ SHADE	☐ OTHER

FERTILISERS & EQUIPMENT

-	-
-	-

PLANTING INSTRUCTIONS

WATER REQUIREMENTS

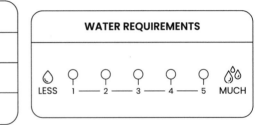

LESS 1 — 2 — 3 — 4 — 5 MUCH

CARE INSTRUCTIONS

STARTED FROM

☐ SEED	☐ PLANT

RATING

🌶️ SIZE	☆☆☆☆☆
🍓 COLOR	☆☆☆☆☆
🍇 TASTE	☆☆☆☆☆

SCIENTIFIC CLASS

☐ VEGETABLE	☐ FRUIT
☐ HERB	☐ FLOWER
☐ SHRUB	☐ TREE
☐ ANNUAL	☐ BIENNIAL
☐ PERENNIAL	☐ SEEDLING

GARDEN LAYOUT

NAME

LOCATION

SUPPLIER

PRICE

DATES

GERMINATED

PLANTED

HARVESTED

LIGHT LEVEL

☐ SUN   ☐ PARTIAL SUN

☐ SHADE   ☐ OTHER

FERTILISERS & EQUIPMENT

-	-
-	-

PLANTING INSTRUCTIONS

WATER REQUIREMENTS

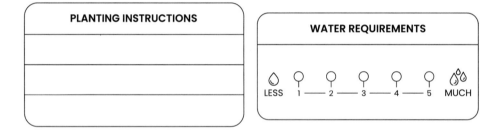

LESS 1 —— 2 —— 3 —— 4 —— 5 MUCH

CARE INSTRUCTIONS

STARTED FROM

☐ SEED   ☐ PLANT

SCIENTIFIC CLASS

☐ VEGETABLE	☐ FRUIT
☐ HERB	☐ FLOWER
☐ SHRUB	☐ TREE
☐ ANNUAL	☐ BIENNIAL
☐ PERENNIAL	☐ SEEDLING

RATING

SIZE	☆☆☆☆☆
COLOR	☆☆☆☆☆
TASTE	☆☆☆☆☆

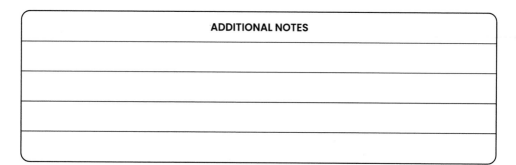

GARDEN LAYOUT

NAME

LOCATION

SUPPLIER

PRICE

DATES

GERMINATED

PLANTED

HARVESTED

LIGHT LEVEL

☐ SUN   ☐ PARTIAL SUN

☐ SHADE   ☐ OTHER

FERTILISERS & EQUIPMENT

-	-
-	-

PLANTING INSTRUCTIONS

WATER REQUIREMENTS

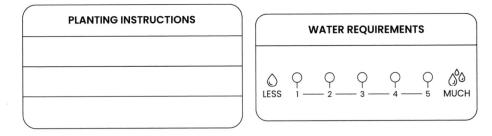

LESS 1 — 2 — 3 — 4 — 5 MUCH

CARE INSTRUCTIONS

STARTED FROM

☐ SEED   ☐ PLANT

SCIENTIFIC CLASS

☐ VEGETABLE	☐ FRUIT
☐ HERB	☐ FLOWER
☐ SHRUB	☐ TREE
☐ ANNUAL	☐ BIENNIAL
☐ PERENNIAL	☐ SEEDLING

RATING

SIZE   ☆☆☆☆☆

COLOR   ☆☆☆☆☆

TASTE   ☆☆☆☆☆

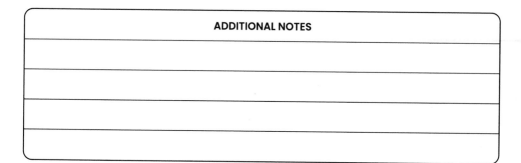

ADDITIONAL NOTES

GARDEN LAYOUT

NAME

LOCATION

SUPPLIER

PRICE

DATES

GERMINATED

PLANTED

HARVESTED

LIGHT LEVEL

☐ SUN   ☐ PARTIAL SUN

☐ SHADE   ☐ OTHER

FERTILISERS & EQUIPMENT

-	-
-	-

PLANTING INSTRUCTIONS

WATER REQUIREMENTS

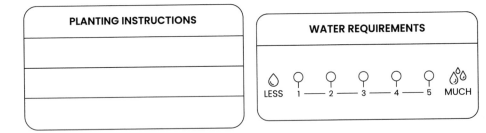

LESS 1 —— 2 —— 3 —— 4 —— 5 MUCH

CARE INSTRUCTIONS

STARTED FROM

☐ SEED   ☐ PLANT

SCIENTIFIC CLASS

☐ VEGETABLE	☐ FRUIT
☐ HERB	☐ FLOWER
☐ SHRUB	☐ TREE
☐ ANNUAL	☐ BIENNIAL
☐ PERENNIAL	☐ SEEDLING

RATING

SIZE   ☆☆☆☆☆

COLOR   ☆☆☆☆☆

TASTE   ☆☆☆☆☆

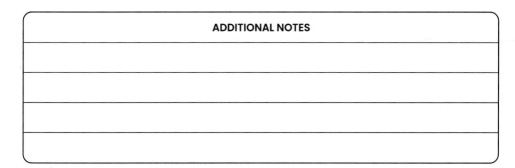

ADDITIONAL NOTES

GARDEN LAYOUT

NAME

LOCATION

SUPPLIER

PRICE

DATES

GERMINATED

PLANTED

HARVESTED

LIGHT LEVEL

| ☐ SUN | ☐ PARTIAL SUN |
| ☐ SHADE | ☐ OTHER |

FERTILISERS & EQUIPMENT

PLANTING INSTRUCTIONS

WATER REQUIREMENTS

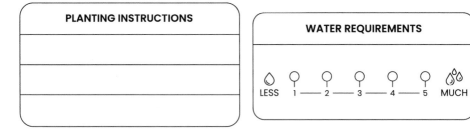

LESS   1 — 2 — 3 — 4 — 5   MUCH

CARE INSTRUCTIONS

STARTED FROM

| ☐ SEED | ☐ PLANT |

SCIENTIFIC CLASS

☐ VEGETABLE	☐ FRUIT
☐ HERB	☐ FLOWER
☐ SHRUB	☐ TREE
☐ ANNUAL	☐ BIENNIAL
☐ PERENNIAL	☐ SEEDLING

RATING

SIZE	☆☆☆☆☆
COLOR	☆☆☆☆☆
TASTE	☆☆☆☆☆

GARDEN LAYOUT

NAME

LOCATION

SUPPLIER

PRICE

DATES

GERMINATED

PLANTED

HARVESTED

LIGHT LEVEL

☐ SUN   ☐ PARTIAL SUN

☐ SHADE   ☐ OTHER

FERTILISERS & EQUIPMENT

-	-
-	-

PLANTING INSTRUCTIONS

WATER REQUIREMENTS

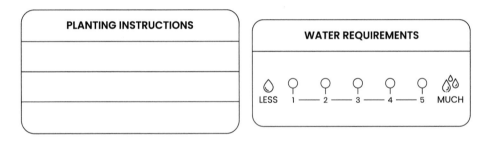

LESS   1 —— 2 —— 3 —— 4 —— 5   MUCH

CARE INSTRUCTIONS

STARTED FROM

☐ SEED	☐ PLANT

SCIENTIFIC CLASS

☐ VEGETABLE	☐ FRUIT
☐ HERB	☐ FLOWER
☐ SHRUB	☐ TREE
☐ ANNUAL	☐ BIENNIAL
☐ PERENNIAL	☐ SEEDLING

RATING

SIZE	☆☆☆☆☆
COLOR	☆☆☆☆☆
TASTE	☆☆☆☆☆

ADDITIONAL NOTES

GARDEN LAYOUT

NAME
LOCATION
SUPPLIER
PRICE

DATES
GERMINATED
PLANTED
HARVESTED

LIGHT LEVEL

☐ SUN	☐ PARTIAL SUN
☐ SHADE	☐ OTHER

FERTILISERS & EQUIPMENT

-	-
-	-

PLANTING INSTRUCTIONS

WATER REQUIREMENTS

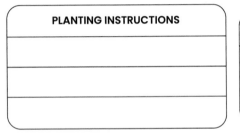

LESS 1 — 2 — 3 — 4 — 5 MUCH

CARE INSTRUCTIONS

STARTED FROM

☐ SEED	☐ PLANT

SCIENTIFIC CLASS

☐ VEGETABLE	☐ FRUIT
☐ HERB	☐ FLOWER
☐ SHRUB	☐ TREE
☐ ANNUAL	☐ BIENNIAL
☐ PERENNIAL	☐ SEEDLING

RATING

SIZE	☆☆☆☆☆
COLOR	☆☆☆☆☆
TASTE	☆☆☆☆☆

ADDITIONAL NOTES

GARDEN LAYOUT

NAME

LOCATION

SUPPLIER

PRICE

DATES

GERMINATED

PLANTED

HARVESTED

LIGHT LEVEL

☐ SUN ☐ PARTIAL SUN

☐ SHADE ☐ OTHER

FERTILISERS & EQUIPMENT

-	-
-	-

PLANTING INSTRUCTIONS

WATER REQUIREMENTS

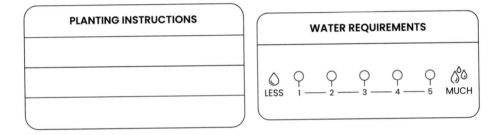

LESS 1 — 2 — 3 — 4 — 5 MUCH

CARE INSTRUCTIONS

STARTED FROM

☐ SEED ☐ PLANT

SCIENTIFIC CLASS

☐ VEGETABLE	☐ FRUIT
☐ HERB	☐ FLOWER
☐ SHRUB	☐ TREE
☐ ANNUAL	☐ BIENNIAL
☐ PERENNIAL	☐ SEEDLING

RATING

SIZE ☆☆☆☆☆

COLOR ☆☆☆☆☆

TASTE ☆☆☆☆☆

ADDITIONAL NOTES

GARDEN LAYOUT

NAME

LOCATION

SUPPLIER

PRICE

DATES

GERMINATED

PLANTED

HARVESTED

LIGHT LEVEL

☐ SUN   ☐ PARTIAL SUN

☐ SHADE   ☐ OTHER

FERTILISERS & EQUIPMENT

-	-
-	-

PLANTING INSTRUCTIONS

WATER REQUIREMENTS

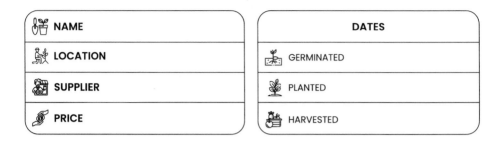

LESS   1 —— 2 —— 3 —— 4 —— 5   MUCH

CARE INSTRUCTIONS

STARTED FROM

☐ SEED   ☐ PLANT

SCIENTIFIC CLASS

☐ VEGETABLE	☐ FRUIT
☐ HERB	☐ FLOWER
☐ SHRUB	☐ TREE
☐ ANNUAL	☐ BIENNIAL
☐ PERENNIAL	☐ SEEDLING

RATING

SIZE   ☆☆☆☆☆

COLOR   ☆☆☆☆☆

TASTE   ☆☆☆☆☆

GARDEN LAYOUT

NAME

LOCATION

SUPPLIER

PRICE

DATES

GERMINATED

PLANTED

HARVESTED

LIGHT LEVEL

☐ SUN ☐ PARTIAL SUN

☐ SHADE ☐ OTHER

FERTILISERS & EQUIPMENT

-	-
-	-

PLANTING INSTRUCTIONS

WATER REQUIREMENTS

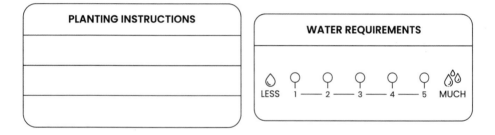

LESS 1 — 2 — 3 — 4 — 5 MUCH

CARE INSTRUCTIONS

STARTED FROM

☐ SEED ☐ PLANT

SCIENTIFIC CLASS

☐ VEGETABLE ☐ FRUIT

☐ HERB ☐ FLOWER

☐ SHRUB ☐ TREE

☐ ANNUAL ☐ BIENNIAL

☐ PERENNIAL ☐ SEEDLING

RATING

SIZE ☆☆☆☆☆

COLOR ☆☆☆☆☆

TASTE ☆☆☆☆☆

ADDITIONAL NOTES

GARDEN LAYOUT

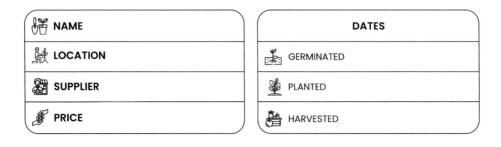

NAME	**DATES**
LOCATION	GERMINATED
SUPPLIER	PLANTED
PRICE	HARVESTED

LIGHT LEVEL

☐ SUN	☐ PARTIAL SUN
☐ SHADE	☐ OTHER

FERTILISERS & EQUIPMENT

-	-
-	-

PLANTING INSTRUCTIONS

WATER REQUIREMENTS

LESS 1 — 2 — 3 — 4 — 5 MUCH

CARE INSTRUCTIONS

STARTED FROM

☐ SEED	☐ PLANT

RATING

🌱 SIZE	☆☆☆☆☆
COLOR	☆☆☆☆☆
TASTE	☆☆☆☆☆

SCIENTIFIC CLASS

☐ VEGETABLE	☐ FRUIT
☐ HERB	☐ FLOWER
☐ SHRUB	☐ TREE
☐ ANNUAL	☐ BIENNIAL
☐ PERENNIAL	☐ SEEDLING

GARDEN LAYOUT

NAME		DATES
LOCATION		GERMINATED
SUPPLIER		PLANTED
PRICE		HARVESTED

LIGHT LEVEL

☐ SUN	☐ PARTIAL SUN
☐ SHADE	☐ OTHER

FERTILISERS & EQUIPMENT

-	-
-	-

PLANTING INSTRUCTIONS

WATER REQUIREMENTS

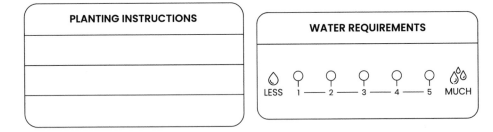

LESS   1 — 2 — 3 — 4 — 5   MUCH

CARE INSTRUCTIONS

STARTED FROM

☐ SEED	☐ PLANT

RATING

🌶 SIZE	☆☆☆☆☆
🍎 COLOR	☆☆☆☆☆
🍇 TASTE	☆☆☆☆☆

SCIENTIFIC CLASS

☐ VEGETABLE	☐ FRUIT
☐ HERB	☐ FLOWER
☐ SHRUB	☐ TREE
☐ ANNUAL	☐ BIENNIAL
☐ PERENNIAL	☐ SEEDLING

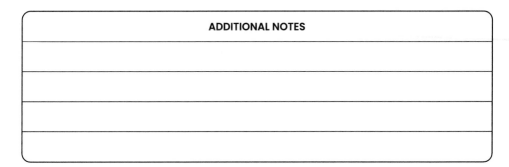

ADDITIONAL NOTES

GARDEN LAYOUT

NAME
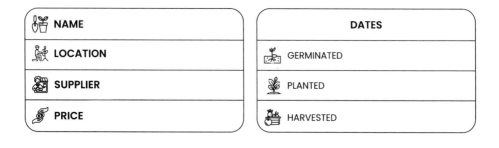

NAME	
LOCATION	
SUPPLIER	
PRICE	

DATES

GERMINATED	
PLANTED	
HARVESTED	

LIGHT LEVEL

☐ SUN	☐ PARTIAL SUN
☐ SHADE	☐ OTHER

FERTILISERS & EQUIPMENT

-	-
-	-

PLANTING INSTRUCTIONS

WATER REQUIREMENTS

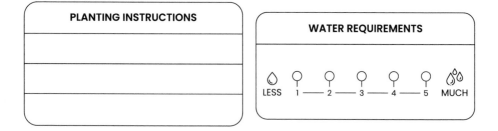

LESS 1 — 2 — 3 — 4 — 5 MUCH

CARE INSTRUCTIONS

STARTED FROM

☐ SEED	☐ PLANT

RATING

🏷 SIZE	☆☆☆☆☆
COLOR	☆☆☆☆☆
TASTE	☆☆☆☆☆

SCIENTIFIC CLASS

☐ VEGETABLE	☐ FRUIT
☐ HERB	☐ FLOWER
☐ SHRUB	☐ TREE
☐ ANNUAL	☐ BIENNIAL
☐ PERENNIAL	☐ SEEDLING

ADDITIONAL NOTES

GARDEN LAYOUT

NAME

LOCATION

SUPPLIER

PRICE

DATES

GERMINATED

PLANTED

HARVESTED

LIGHT LEVEL

☐ SUN ☐ PARTIAL SUN

☐ SHADE ☐ OTHER

FERTILISERS & EQUIPMENT

PLANTING INSTRUCTIONS

WATER REQUIREMENTS

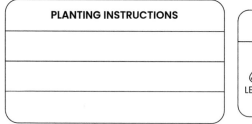

LESS 1 — 2 — 3 — 4 — 5 MUCH

CARE INSTRUCTIONS

STARTED FROM

☐ SEED ☐ PLANT

SCIENTIFIC CLASS

☐ VEGETABLE ☐ FRUIT

☐ HERB ☐ FLOWER

☐ SHRUB ☐ TREE

☐ ANNUAL ☐ BIENNIAL

☐ PERENNIAL ☐ SEEDLING

RATING

SIZE ☆☆☆☆☆

COLOR ☆☆☆☆☆

TASTE ☆☆☆☆☆

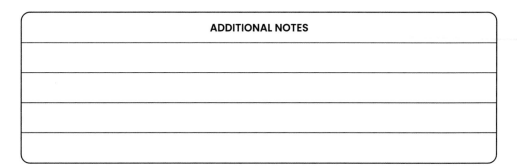

ADDITIONAL NOTES

GARDEN LAYOUT

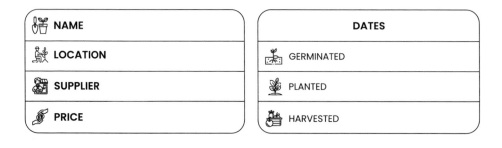

NAME	DATES	
LOCATION	GERMINATED	
SUPPLIER	PLANTED	
PRICE	HARVESTED	

LIGHT LEVEL

☐ SUN	☐ PARTIAL SUN
☐ SHADE	☐ OTHER

FERTILISERS & EQUIPMENT

-	-
-	-

PLANTING INSTRUCTIONS

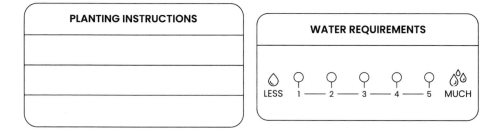

WATER REQUIREMENTS

LESS 1 — 2 — 3 — 4 — 5 MUCH

CARE INSTRUCTIONS

STARTED FROM

☐ SEED	☐ PLANT

RATING

SIZE	☆☆☆☆☆
COLOR	☆☆☆☆☆
TASTE	☆☆☆☆☆

SCIENTIFIC CLASS

☐ VEGETABLE	☐ FRUIT
☐ HERB	☐ FLOWER
☐ SHRUB	☐ TREE
☐ ANNUAL	☐ BIENNIAL
☐ PERENNIAL	☐ SEEDLING

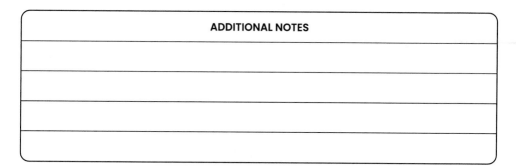

GARDEN LAYOUT

NAME

LOCATION

SUPPLIER

PRICE

DATES

GERMINATED

PLANTED

HARVESTED

LIGHT LEVEL

☐ SUN	☐ PARTIAL SUN
☐ SHADE	☐ OTHER

FERTILISERS & EQUIPMENT

-	-
-	-

PLANTING INSTRUCTIONS

WATER REQUIREMENTS

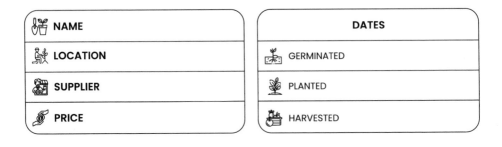

LESS   1 —— 2 —— 3 —— 4 —— 5   MUCH

CARE INSTRUCTIONS

STARTED FROM

☐ SEED	☐ PLANT

RATING

SIZE	☆☆☆☆☆
COLOR	☆☆☆☆☆
TASTE	☆☆☆☆☆

SCIENTIFIC CLASS

☐ VEGETABLE	☐ FRUIT
☐ HERB	☐ FLOWER
☐ SHRUB	☐ TREE
☐ ANNUAL	☐ BIENNIAL
☐ PERENNIAL	☐ SEEDLING

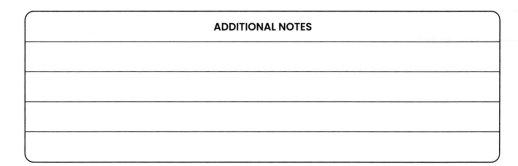

ADDITIONAL NOTES

GARDEN LAYOUT

NAME

LOCATION

SUPPLIER

PRICE

DATES

GERMINATED

PLANTED

HARVESTED

LIGHT LEVEL

| ☐ SUN | ☐ PARTIAL SUN |
| ☐ SHADE | ☐ OTHER |

FERTILISERS & EQUIPMENT

PLANTING INSTRUCTIONS

WATER REQUIREMENTS

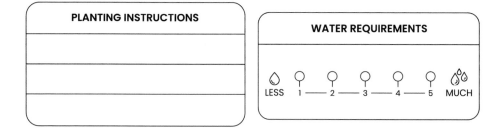

LESS 1 — 2 — 3 — 4 — 5 MUCH

CARE INSTRUCTIONS

STARTED FROM

| ☐ SEED | ☐ PLANT |

RATING

🪴 SIZE	☆☆☆☆☆
🍎 COLOR	☆☆☆☆☆
🍓 TASTE	☆☆☆☆☆

SCIENTIFIC CLASS

☐ VEGETABLE	☐ FRUIT
☐ HERB	☐ FLOWER
☐ SHRUB	☐ TREE
☐ ANNUAL	☐ BIENNIAL
☐ PERENNIAL	☐ SEEDLING

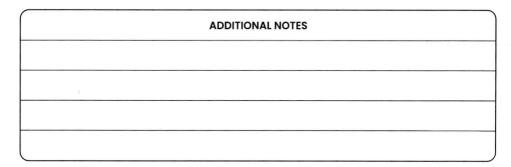

GARDEN LAYOUT

NAME

LOCATION

SUPPLIER

PRICE

DATES

GERMINATED

PLANTED

HARVESTED

LIGHT LEVEL

☐ SUN ☐ PARTIAL SUN

☐ SHADE ☐ OTHER

FERTILISERS & EQUIPMENT

-	-
-	-

PLANTING INSTRUCTIONS

WATER REQUIREMENTS

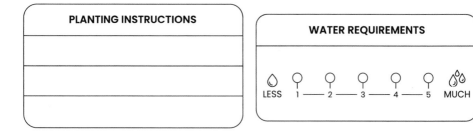

LESS 1 — 2 — 3 — 4 — 5 MUCH

CARE INSTRUCTIONS

STARTED FROM

☐ SEED ☐ PLANT

RATING

🌶 SIZE	☆☆☆☆☆
🍎 COLOR	☆☆☆☆☆
🫐 TASTE	☆☆☆☆☆

SCIENTIFIC CLASS

☐ VEGETABLE	☐ FRUIT
☐ HERB	☐ FLOWER
☐ SHRUB	☐ TREE
☐ ANNUAL	☐ BIENNIAL
☐ PERENNIAL	☐ SEEDLING

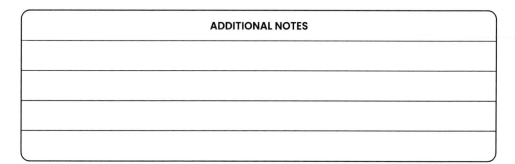

ADDITIONAL NOTES

GARDEN LAYOUT

NAME

LOCATION

SUPPLIER

PRICE

DATES

GERMINATED

PLANTED

HARVESTED

LIGHT LEVEL

☐ SUN ☐ PARTIAL SUN

☐ SHADE ☐ OTHER

FERTILISERS & EQUIPMENT

-	-
-	-

PLANTING INSTRUCTIONS

WATER REQUIREMENTS

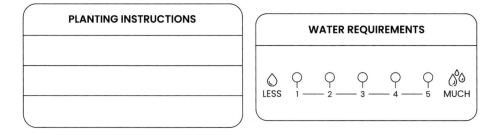

LESS 1 — 2 — 3 — 4 — 5 MUCH

CARE INSTRUCTIONS

STARTED FROM

☐ SEED ☐ PLANT

RATING

🌱 SIZE	☆☆☆☆☆
🍅 COLOR	☆☆☆☆☆
🍓 TASTE	☆☆☆☆☆

SCIENTIFIC CLASS

☐ VEGETABLE	☐ FRUIT
☐ HERB	☐ FLOWER
☐ SHRUB	☐ TREE
☐ ANNUAL	☐ BIENNIAL
☐ PERENNIAL	☐ SEEDLING

ADDITIONAL NOTES

GARDEN LAYOUT

NAME

LOCATION

SUPPLIER

PRICE

DATES

GERMINATED

PLANTED

HARVESTED

LIGHT LEVEL

SUN	PARTIAL SUN
SHADE	OTHER

FERTILISERS & EQUIPMENT

-	-
-	-

PLANTING INSTRUCTIONS

WATER REQUIREMENTS

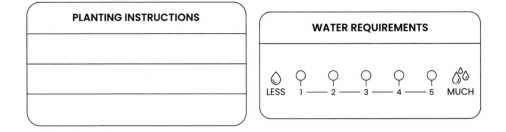

LESS 1 — 2 — 3 — 4 — 5 MUCH

CARE INSTRUCTIONS

STARTED FROM

SEED	PLANT

SCIENTIFIC CLASS

VEGETABLE	FRUIT
HERB	FLOWER
SHRUB	TREE
ANNUAL	BIENNIAL
PERENNIAL	SEEDLING

RATING

SIZE	☆☆☆☆☆
COLOR	☆☆☆☆☆
TASTE	☆☆☆☆☆

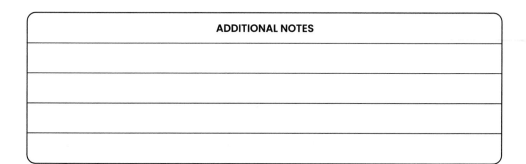

ADDITIONAL NOTES

GARDEN LAYOUT

NAME		DATES	
LOCATION		GERMINATED	
SUPPLIER		PLANTED	
PRICE		HARVESTED	

LIGHT LEVEL

☐ SUN	☐ PARTIAL SUN
☐ SHADE	☐ OTHER

FERTILISERS & EQUIPMENT

-	-
-	-

PLANTING INSTRUCTIONS

WATER REQUIREMENTS

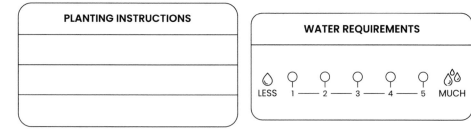

LESS 1 — 2 — 3 — 4 — 5 MUCH

CARE INSTRUCTIONS

STARTED FROM

☐ SEED	☐ PLANT

SCIENTIFIC CLASS

☐ VEGETABLE	☐ FRUIT
☐ HERB	☐ FLOWER
☐ SHRUB	☐ TREE
☐ ANNUAL	☐ BIENNIAL
☐ PERENNIAL	☐ SEEDLING

RATING

SIZE	☆☆☆☆☆
COLOR	☆☆☆☆☆
TASTE	☆☆☆☆☆

ADDITIONAL NOTES

GARDEN LAYOUT

NAME

LOCATION

SUPPLIER

PRICE

DATES

GERMINATED

PLANTED

HARVESTED

LIGHT LEVEL

- [ ] SUN
- [ ] PARTIAL SUN
- [ ] SHADE
- [ ] OTHER

FERTILISERS & EQUIPMENT

-	-
-	-

PLANTING INSTRUCTIONS

WATER REQUIREMENTS

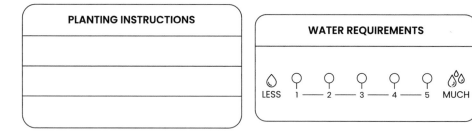

LESS 1 — 2 — 3 — 4 — 5 MUCH

CARE INSTRUCTIONS

STARTED FROM

- [ ] SEED
- [ ] PLANT

SCIENTIFIC CLASS

[ ] VEGETABLE	[ ] FRUIT
[ ] HERB	[ ] FLOWER
[ ] SHRUB	[ ] TREE
[ ] ANNUAL	[ ] BIENNIAL
[ ] PERENNIAL	[ ] SEEDLING

RATING

SIZE	☆☆☆☆☆
COLOR	☆☆☆☆☆
TASTE	☆☆☆☆☆

GARDEN LAYOUT

Sed Publishing

Please leave us a review
because we would love to know your thoughts

Check out our other logbooks just search

Sed Publishing 🔍

Follow us on

Sed Publishing

Sed Publishing

Copyright © 2021 Sed Publishing.
All rights reserved .

Made in the USA
Thornton, CO
05/25/23 18:01:05

c386d5e9-7926-47d8-ac3b-624a54cd82caR01